# Naturally Sugar-Free

Vegetarian and Weeknight Dinners Cookbook

All Rights Reserved. No part of this publication may be reproduced in any form or by any means, including scanning, photocopying, or otherwise without prior written permission of the copyright holder. Copyright © 2014

# Introduction

The modern vegetarian diet is often shockingly unhealthy – added sugar hides in processed soy products, bread, salad dressings, prepackaged dinners and many other sneaky places. To make matters worse, many people don't know how to give flavour to their meatless culinary creations without adding sugar or fat. If this description sounds like you, don't despair: you are not alone! This is why we have created this cookbook with 30 naturally flavourful vegetarian recipes. You don't have to add tons of sugar to create a stunning meal. In fact, wholesome and healthy ingredients such as fruits, veggies, nuts and eggs can allow endless creative possibilities for tasty meals that you can feel great about serving to your loved ones.

# Table of Contents

Spicy Kale Quiche

Eggplant with Pesto Topping

Spicy Zucchini Eggplant Dine

Lettuce Nut Salad

Eggplant with Red Sauce

Sweet Potatoes Roast

Pepper Quiche

"Green Bean" Casserole

Mushroom Masala

Easy Matzo Ball Soup

Butternut Squash Soup

Mexican Tomato Soup

Creamy "Cheesy" Broccoli Soup

Pita Bites

Simple Gazpacho + Tortilla Chips

Grain-Free Tortillas

Sugar-Free Veggie Burger

- Soft Burger Buns
- Egg Salad Sandwich
- Sandwich Bread
- Sugar-Free Orange Kelp Noodle Salad
- Zucchini Salad with Sundried Tomato Sauce
- Quick Raw Avocado Slaw
- Vegetarian Texas Chili
- Caesar Salad
- Spiced Walnut Autumn Salad
- Pecan Apricot Spinach Salad
- Southern Style Egg Salad
- Pesto Tomato Caprese
- Cashew Crunch Kelp Noodle Salad
- Dill Stuffed Tomatoes
- Squash Blossom Stuffers
- Sugar-Free Indian Egg Fried Rice

# Spicy Kale Quiche

Prep time: 10 minutes

Cook time: 15 minutes

Serves: 4

INGREDIENTS

8 cage-free eggs

2 tbsp extra virgin olive oil

1 7oz bag of Kale greens

1 shallot

¼ tsp chipotle chili pepper powder

2 cloves garlic

½ lemon

2 tbsp coconut oil

¼ tbsp ground black pepper

INSTRUCTIONS

1. Place a steamer basket in the bottom of a large pot and fill with water; if you see water rise above the bottom of the basket, pour some out. Bring the water to a boil.
2. Wash the kale and remove the stems. Mince the garlic and shallot and squeeze the juice from the lemon into a bowl.
3. In a large pan, add the eggs and extra virgin olive oil. Mixing in the chipotle chili pepper powder, scramble the eggs, breaking them up until they form many small pieces, tender yet firm.
4. Place the kale in the pot and steam until tender and bright-green.

5. Remove the kale from the pot and combine with the eggs. Add the garlic, shallot and lemon juice, drizzle the coconut oil over top and add the ground black pepper. Mix and stir thoroughly.
6. Serve immediately or chill 20 minutes and then serve.

# Eggplant with Pesto Topping

Prep time: 10 minutes

Cook time: 8 minutes

Serves: 4

INGREDIENTS

1 large, thick eggplant

6-8 tomatoes

4 tbsp olive oil

¼ cup fresh basil

2 cloves garlic

INSTRUCTIONS

1. Preheat the grill. Slice the eggplant lengthwise into ½" thick slices, or ensuring that you have 4 slices. Slice the tomatoes into ¼" thick slices. Combine 4 tbsp olive oil with basil and garlic in a food processor and puree together.
2. Grill the eggplant until browned, turning once, about 3-4 minutes per side.
3. Remove eggplant from the grill and lay the tomato slices out over each piece. Top with the pesto puree and serve.

# Spicy Zucchini Eggplant Dine

Prep time: 15 minutes

Cook time: 20 minutes

Serves: 4

INGREDIENTS

3 small zucchini

1 eggplant

2 green peppers

6 tomatoes

1 onion

2 medium carrots

1 four-inch sweet orange pepper

1 cup water

1 tbsp extra virgin olive oil

INSTRUCTIONS

1. Using a julienne peeler, peel zucchini, eggplant and green peppers. Green peppers may be too tough for a julienne peeler, in which case try to simulate the effect of one using a knife. Combine the above in a pan with extra virgin olive oil and saute over medium heat, stirring, for 5 minutes.
2. Meanwhile, cut tomatoes into quarters, carrots into ½" thick slices, dice sweet pepper and dice onion. In a saucepan, combine the above with water and cook over medium heat until carrot is tender,

about 15 minutes. Once finished, blend using an immersion blender, or pour into a blender and puree.
3. Pour the sauce over the zucchini, eggplant and peppers and serve.

# Lettuce Nut Salad

Prep time: 10 min

Cook time: 6-8 minutes

Serves: 4

INGREDIENTS

1 7oz bag of Romaine lettuce

1 cup strawberries

1 cup blueberries

1 cup kiwi

½ cup almonds

½ cup walnuts

2 cups coconut milk

1 tbsp arrowroot

1 tsp cinnamon

¼ tsp chipotle chili pepper powder

INSTRUCTIONS

1. Dice the fruits. In a saucepan, combine coconut milk, arrowroot, cinnamon and chipotle chili pepper powder over medium heat. Cook, stirring, for 4 minutes. Add the walnuts and almonds to the sauce and continue cooking until slightly thick.
2. Combine lettuce and fruit in a bowl and drizzle the sauce over the top. Serve immediately or chill 20 minutes and then serve.

# Eggplant with Red Sauce

Prep time: 10 minutes

Cook time: 8 minutes

Serves: 2

INGREDIENTS

½ large eggplant cut lengthwise

4 asparagus stalks

2 cloves garlic

1 yellow tomato

2 tsp fresh cilantro

2 tbsp extra virgin olive oil

1 cup organic red sauce

INSTRUCTIONS

1. In a medium saucepan, heat the red sauce on low and keep hot.
2. Slice the eggplant into ½ inch slices, 8 slices total. Heat 1 ½ extra virgin olive oil in a frying pan on medium heat. Cook the eggplant two minutes on one side and another two minutes on the other side. Transfer to a plate.
3. Add ½ tbsp to the pan. Slice the garlic. Rinse the asparagus and cut each asparagus stalk into 3 equal lengths.
4. Add garlic and asparagus to pan and sautee until asparagus is tender.
5. Dice yellow tomato and cilantro and mix together.

6. Place four slices of eggplant on each plate. Spoon red sauce over each slice. Cover with tomato/cilantro mixture and evenly distribute asparagus and garlic cloves.
7. Serve.

# Sweet Potatoes Roast

Prep time: 10 minutes

Cook time: 30 minutes

INGREDIENTS

3 sweet potatoes

¼ cup extra virgin olive oil

¼ tsp Celtic sea salt

¼ tsp smoked paprika

INSTRUCTIONS

1. Preheat oven to 500 degrees.
2. Peel the potatoes and cut them into small wedges. In a large bowl, combine potato wedges, extra virgin olive oil, Celtic sea salt and smoked paprika. Mix well until all wedges are coated in all ingredients.
3. Place on a baking sheet and bake for 30 minutes, turning once halfway through, and continue cooking until they are well browned.
4. Remove from oven and let cool. Serve.

# Pepper Quiche

Prep time: 5 minutes

Cook time: 3-6 minutes

INGREDIENTS

2 cage-free eggs

1 small onion

1 clove garlic

½ red bell pepper

1 tbsp extra virgin olive oil

¼ tsp smoked paprika

¼ tsp ground black pepper

INSTRUCTIONS
1. Finely chop onion, garlic and red bell pepper.
2. Pour extra virgin olive oil into a pan over medium heat.
3. Crack eggs and pour into a small bowl. Combine with onion, garlic and red bell pepper and whisk until mixed together.
4. Pour contents of bowl into pan and add smoked paprika and ground black pepper. Scramble until desired doneness.
5. Serve.

# "Green Bean" Casserole

Prep Time: 5 minutes

Cook Time: 20 minutes

Servings: 12

INGREDIENTS

*Casserole*

4 cups asparagus

2 cups button mushrooms

1 cup nut milk

1/2 cup cegetable stock

2 tablespoons tapioca flour

1 teaspoon ground white pepper (or ground black pepper)

1 teaspoon garlic powder

1 teaspoon onion powder

*Crispy Onions*

1/2 cup almond meal

1/2 medium onion (yellow or white)

1 cage-free egg

1 teaspoon paprika

1 teaspoon onion powder

1/4 teaspoon ground black pepper

1 teaspoon Celtic sea salt

Coconut oil (for cooking)

INSTRUCTIONS

1. Preheat oven to 350 degrees F. Bring medium pot of water plus 1/2 teaspoon salt to a boil.
2. For *Casserole*, cut asparagus stalks into quarters. Add to boiling water for about 3 - 4 minutes, until tender but not mushy. Drain and shock in ice bath to stop cooking an preserve color. Set aside.
3. Add tapioca flour and vegetable stock to large pan and heat over medium-high heat. Whisk until smooth, then add nut milk, white pepper, garlic and onion powder.
4. Slice mushrooms and add to pan. Stir and thicken about 8 minutes, until thick and creamy.
5. Add asparagus to pan and stir to coat. Pour into baking or casserole dish and bake about 20 minutes, until heated through. Remove from oven and let cool BOUT 5 minutes.
6. Heat medium pan on medium-high heat and coat with coconut oil.
7. For *Crispy Onions*, whisk egg in medium bowl. In shallow dish, mix almond meal with spices.
8. Peel and slice onion. Toss onions in beaten egg, then in seasoned almond meal to coat. Add to hot oiled pan and fry until crispy and golden brown, about 1 - 2 minutes.
9. Drain *Crispy Onions* on paper towel, then sprinkle over *Casserole*. Serve warm.

# Mushroom Masala

Prep Time: 10 minutes

Cook Time: 25 minutes

Servings: 8

INGREDIENTS

1 head cauliflower

1 1/2 cups tomato purée (or tomato sauce)

1 pint (2 cups) mushrooms

1 onion

1 chili pepper

1 /2 green bell pepper

1 large garlic clove

1 inch piece fresh ginger

2 teaspoons coriander leaves (optional)

1 teaspoon garam masala

1/2 teaspoon cayenne pepper

1/2 teaspoon ground coriander

1/2 teaspoon Celtic sea salt

3 tablespoons coconut oil or ghee

INSTRUCTIONS

1. Roughly chop cauliflower, then rice cauliflower in food processor, or mince. Add to medium pot with enough water to cover. Heat pot over medium heat and cook until just tender, about 8 minutes. Drain and transfer to serving dish.

2. Heat medium pan over medium heat. Add oil or butter to hot pan.
3. Peel and finely dice onions. Remove seeds, veins and stem from bell pepper and dice. Slice chili pepper. Peel and mince garlic and onion. Add to hot oiled pan and sauté about 5 minutes.
4. Slice mushrooms and add to pan with tomato, salt and spices. Finely chop coriander leaves and add to pan (optional). Sauté and let simmer about 10 - 12 minutes, stirring occasionally.
5. Transfer to serving dish and serve hot with cauliflower rice.

# Easy Matzo Ball Soup

Prep Time: 5 minutes*

Cook Time: 10 minutes

Servings: 6

INGREDIENTS

6 cups vegetable stock

2 cups almond flour

4 cage-free egg yolks

1/4 teaspoon ground white pepper (or ground black pepper)

2 teaspoons Celtic sea salt

INSTRUCTIONS

1. In a medium bowl, beat eggs,1 teaspoon salt and pepper until light and frothy, about 2 minutes. Sift almond flour into bowl and mix until dough comes together.
2. *Cover dough with parchment, if preferred, and refrigerate 2 - 4 hours.
3. Add 1 teaspoon salt to large pot of water and bring to boil. Add vegetable stock to medium pot and heat over medium heat.
4. Remove dough from refrigerator and roll into balls. Carefully place dough balls in boiling water. Reduce heat to low, cover and simmer 20 minutes, until cooked through.
5. Transfer matzo balls to serving dish with slotted spoon. Ladle heated vegetable stock over matzo balls and serve hot.

# Butternut Squash Soup

Prep Time: 10 minutes

Cook Time: 1 hour

Servings: 4

## INGREDIENTS

1 medium-large butternut squash (about 2 cups diced)

2 cups veggie stock

1/2 cup coconut milk (optional)

1/2 onion (white, yellow or sweet)

1/2 large carrot

1/2 celery stalk

1/2 teaspoon ground coriander (optional)

1 cinnamon stick

Ground black pepper, to taste

Celtic sea salt, to taste

2 tablespoons shelled pumpkin seeds (toasted or raw)

2 tablespoons ghee (or coconut oil)

2 tablespoons coconut oil

## INSTRUCTIONS

1. Heat oven to 375 degrees F. Heat medium cast iron pan over medium-high heat. Add butter to hot oiled pan.
2. Peel squash and remove seeds. Dice and add to hot oiled pan with salt and pepper, to taste. Sauté until golden, about 3 - 4 minutes.

Place pan in oven and roast until browned on all sides, about 15 minutes.

3. Heat medium pot over medium-low heat. Add coconut oil to hot pot.
4. Peel and dice onion, celery and carrot. Add to hot oiled pot with cinnamon stick, salt and pepper to taste. Sauté until soft but not browned, about 10 minutes.
5. Remove squash from oven and let cool slightly. Add food processor or high-speed blender and process until puréed.
6. Add vegetable broth and coriander (optional) to pot. Increase heat to medium and bring to boil. Simmer about 5 minutes.
7. Stir in squash purée and simmer about 10 minutes. Discard cinnamon stick.
8. Add mixture to food processor or high-speed blender and purée until smooth. Or blend with immerse or stick blender until smooth.
9. Transfer mixture back to hot pot and stir in coconut milk (optional). Transfer to serving dish.
10. Sprinkle with pumpkin seeds and cracked black pepper. Serve hot.

# Mexican Tomato Soup

Prep Time: 10 minutes

Cook Time: 40 minutes

Servings: 4

INGREDIENTS

2 cans (14.5 oz) organic crushed tomatoes

2 cans (11.5) organic tomato juice

5 large tomatoes (or 10 plum tomatoes)

1/2 cup coconut milk

1 red bell pepper (or 1/4 cup roasted red peppers, jarred)

1/4 red onion (or yellow or white onion)

2 garlic cloves

1/2 Serrano chili pepper (or other chili pepper) (optional)

1 tablespoon tapioca flour (or arrowroot powder)

2 tablespoons fresh Mexican oregano (or 1 teaspoon dried oregano)

2 large basil leaves

1 teaspoon fresh cracked black pepper (or ground black pepper)

Celtic sea salt, to taste

1 small bunch cilantro (for garnish)

2 tablespoons ghee (or cacao butter, or coconut oil)

INSTRUCTIONS

1. Juice tomatoes and set aside.

2. Roast red bell pepper over stove burner or until broiler, if using. Turn to char on all sides until skins sears. Rub off blackened skin. Cut in half and remove seeds, stem and veins.
3. Heat medium pot over medium-high heat. Add fat to hot pot.
4. Peel onion and garlic. Dice onion, roasted and red pepper. Mince garlic and Serrano pepper (optional). Add to hot oiled pot and sauté until fragrant, about 2 minutes.
5. Add tapioca and coconut milk. Stir to combine. Let cook about 2 minutes.
6. Chiffon (thinly slice) basil. Add to pot with tomato juice, crushed tomatoes, oregano, pepper and salt, to taste. Stir to combine.
7. Bring to simmer, then reduce heat to low. Simmer and reduce about 30 minutes, or until desired consistency is reached.
8. Transfer to serving dish. Chop cilantro and sprinkle over dish for garnish.
9. Serve hot.

# Creamy "Cheesy" Broccoli Soup

Prep Time: 10 minutes

Cook Time: 30 minutes

Servings: 4

INGREDIENTS

1 large head broccoli

2 cups vegetable broth

1 cup nut milk

1/2 cup nutritional yeast

1 medium onion (white or yellow)

2 garlic cloves

1 tablespoon coconut aminos (or liquid aminos or tamari)

1 tablespoon mustard powder

Celtic sea salt, to taste.

1 teaspoon ground white pepper (or 1/2 teaspoon ground black pepper)

2 tablespoons bacon fat (or coconut oil, cacao butterr ghee)

Water

INSTRUCTIONS
1. Heat medium pot over medium heat. Add fat or oil to hot pot.
2. Peel onion and garlic. Chop and add to hot pot. Sauté until fragrant, about 2 minutes.
3. Chop broccoli and add to pot with vegetable broth. Increase heat and bring to boil. Cover and boil about 15 - 20 minutes until broccoli is softened.

4. Pour pot in to food processor or high-speed blender with nutritional yeast, coconut aminos, spices and salt, to taste. Process until smooth, about 1 - 2 minutes. Add enough water to reach desired consistency.
5. Transfer to serving dish and serve immediately.
6. Or add back to pot and heat through over medium heat. Then serve.

# Pita Bites

Prep Time: *5 minutes

Cook Time: 20 minutes

Servings: 1

INGREDIENTS

*Pita Bites*

1 cup tapioca flour/starch

1 teaspoon ground chia seed (or flax meal)

1 egg

2 tablespoons coconut oil

1/4 cup water

1/2 teaspoon baking soda

1/4 teaspoon sea salt

*Almond Hummus*

1 cup skinless almonds

1/3 cup tahini

1 garlic clove

Juice of 1/2 lemon

Zest of 1/2 lemon

1/4 teaspoon sea salt

1/4 cup water

2 tablespoons pine nuts

INSTRUCTIONS
1. *Soak almonds overnight in enough water to cover. Drain and rinse.
2. Preheat oven to 375 degrees F. Cover sheet pan with parchment paper or baking mat. Heat small pot over low heat.
3. For *Pita Bites*, mix 1/3 cup tapioca flour with chia meal, water and 1 tablespoon coconut oil in pot. Stir until mixture comes together. Remove from heat and cool in freezer.
4. In medium bowl, blend remaining tapioca flour, baking soda and salt. Then add egg and remaining oil. Mix until combined.
5. Add cooled chia mixture to bowl and mix to combine. Then remove and knead to form dough.
6. Form large round disk, then use rolling pin to flatten on lined baking sheet. Cut out circles with biscuit cutter or drinking glass, or cut triangles with pizza cutter. Re-roll excess dough and repeat until all dough is used.
7. Arrange pita pieces on sheet pan and place in oven. Bake about 10 minutes. Carefully turn over with spatula and bake another 5 - 7 minutes, or until crisp.
8. Remove from oven and let cool completely. Place in lidded container or sealable lunch bag and serve room temperature.
9. For *Almond Hummus*, add 1/2 of water to all ingredients in food processor or bullet blender and process. Add just enough water to smooth blend.
10. Scrape hummus into lidded container and serve chilled or room temperature with *Pita Bites*.

# Simple Gazpacho + Tortilla Chips

Prep Time: 20 minutes

Cook Time: 10 minutes

Servings: 4

INGREDIENTS

*Grain-Free Tortillas*

*Gazpacho*

2 (11.5 oz) cans organic tomato juice (or 3 cups juiced tomatoes)

4 plum tomatoes

2 red bell peppers

1 red onion

1 cucumber

3 garlic cloves

1/4 cup apple cider vinegar

1/4 cup coconut oil (or 2 tablespoons coconut oil and 2 tablespoons flavorful oil [walnut, almond, sesame, etc.])

1 teaspoon cracked black pepper (or ground black pepper)

1/2 tablespoon sea salt

INSTRUCTIONS

1. Seed cucumber and tomatoes. Seed, stem and vein bell peppers. Peel onion and garlic. Dice veggies, mince garlic, and add to medium serving bowl.

2. Add tomato juice, vinegar, oil, salt and pepper, and mix well. Place in refrigerator.
3. Heat medium pan over medium-high heat and coat with coconut oil.
4. For *Tortilla Chips*, prepare *Grain-Free Tortillas*.
5. Add more coconut oil to hot pan and allow to heat up. Cut tortillas into wedges with pizza cutter or sharp knife.
6. Add tortilla wedges back to hot pan in single layer and cook about 30 seconds on each side, until golden and crisp. Drain on paper towel. Repeat with remaining tortilla wedges.
7. Transfer warm *Tortilla Chips* to serving dish. Serve immediately with chilled *Gazpacho*.

# Grain-Free Tortillas

Prep Time: 5 minutes

Cook Time: 10 minutes

Servings: 2

INGREDIENTS

2 tablespoons almond flour

2 tablespoons coconut flour

1/2 tablespoon flax meal (or ground chia seed)

2 eggs

1/4 cup water (plus extra)

2 tablespoons coconut oil

1/4 teaspoon baking powder

Coconut oil (for cooking)

INSTRUCTIONS

1. Heat medium frying pan over medium-high heat and coat with coconut oil.
2. Whisk together eggs, coconut oil and 1/4 cup water in medium bowl.
3. In separate mixing bowl, blend coconut flour, almond flour, flax or chia seed, and baking powder.
4. Slowly whisk as you pour flourmixture into wet ingredients. If batter appears too thick to spread fairly thin in pan, add up to 4 tablespoon water 1 tablespoon at a time.

5. Use ladle or dry measure cup to pour 1/2 of batter into hot oiled pan. Tilt pan in circular motion as you pour so batter spreads thinly.
6. Cook batter for about 2 minutes or until slightly golden and firm. Flip tortilla with tongs or spatula and cook another 2 minutes. Remove and place on paper towel or parchment.
7. Cook remaining batter for 2 minutes on each side. Re-oil pan as necessary.
8. Fill warm tortillas with meat or veggies of choice and serve warm.

# Sugar-Free Veggie Burger

Prep Time: 5 minutes

Cook Time: 20 minutes

Servings: 4

INGREDIENTS

*Soft Burger Bun*

*Veggie Burger*

2 eggs

1/2 head cauliflower

2 medium carrots

1 small white onion

1 cup walnuts (1/2 cup ground)

1/4 cup almond flour

2 tablespoons tapioca flour

2 tablespoons ground chia seed (or flax meal)

2 cloves garlic

1 teaspoon paprika

1 teaspoon ground black pepper

1 teaspoon sea salt

*Topping*

1 avocado

1 heirloom tomato

1 white onion

2 ribs romaine lettuce (or preferred lettuce)

INSTRUCTIONS

1. Preheat oven to 350 degrees F. Line sheet pan with parchment paper, or lightly coat with coconut oil. Or lightly coat 6 mini round cake pans with coconut oil.
2. Prepare *Soft Burger Buns* and place in oven.
3. While bread bakes, line dish with parchment paper.
4. Add walnuts and almond four to food processor or bullet blender. Process until finely ground. Add to medium mixing bowl.
5. Peel small onion and garlic. Add to processor or blender with cauliflower and carrots. Process until finely ground. Add eggs, tapioca and chia. Process until mixture becomes thickened and has batter-like consistency.
6. Add veggie mixture and spices to mixing bowl. Mix all ingredients together with hands or wooden spoon until fully combined and uniform.
7. Form veggie mixture into 4 patties and place on parchment lined dish. Place in freezer for 10 minutes.
8. Heat medium skillet over medium-high heat and add 1 tablespoon coconut oil.
9. Peel onion. Make 4 thick slices, keeping full ring intact. Using spatula, place full rings into hot oiled pan. Sear 1 minute on each side. Set aside on paper towel to drain.
10. Reduce heat to medium and coat pan with coconut oil.
11. Remove veggie patties from freezer and place in hot oiled pan. Cook 5 minutes, then carefully flip with spatula and cook another 5 minutes.

12. Remove *Soft Burger Bun* from oven and let cool about 5 minutes.
13. Cut lettuce ribs in half. Cut tomato into 4 thick slices. Slice avocado in half, pit and slice flesh in peel.
14. Slice bun in half and place lettuce on bottom bun, followed by tomato slice. Add burger patty, then grilled onion ring. Finish with a few slices of avocado and top bun.
15. Serve immediately.

# Soft Burger Buns

Prep Time: 5 minutes

Cook Time: 15 minutes

Servings: 6

INGREDIENTS

1/4 cup almond flour

1/4 cup coconut flour

4 eggs

2 tablespoons coconut oil

2 tablespoons unsweetened applesauce

1 teaspoon flax meal (or ground chia seed)

1 teaspoon baking powder

1/2 teaspoon sea salt

INSTRUCTIONS

1. Preheat oven to 350 degrees F. Line sheet pan with parchment paper, or lightly coat with coconut oil. Or lightly coat 6 mini round cake pans with coconut oil.
2. Beat eggs, coconut oil and applesauce in medium mixing bowl with hand mixer or whisk.
3. In large mixing bowl, sift together coconut flour, almond flour, flax or chia meal, baking powder and salt. Pour egg mixture into flour mixture and mix until combined.

4. Scoop thick batter onto prepared sheet pan in six 4 inch rounds. Or pour into six prepared mini cake pans for uniformity. Smooth batter with knife or spatula.
5. Place in oven and bake for 12 - 15 minutes, or until tops are firm to the touch and golden.
6. Remove from oven and let cool at least 5 minutes.
7. Slice in half and serve with your favorite patty or filling.

# Egg Salad Sandwich

Prep Time: 5 minutes

Cook Time: 15 minutes

Servings: 2

INGREDIENTS

*Sandwich Bread*

*Avocado Egg Salad*

8 eggs

1 avocado

1/4 cup dill pickle relish

3 tablespoons organic mustard

2 teaspoons paprika

1/2 teaspoon ground black pepper

1/4 teaspoon sea salt

INSTRUCTIONS

1. Preheat oven to 350 degrees F. Lightly coat 6 mini round cake pans or medium loaf pan with coconut oil. Bring medium pot of lightly salted water to a boil.
2. Prepare *Sandwich Bread* and place in oven.
3. While bread bakes, gently add eggs to hot water with tongs and cook about 8 - 10 minutes.
4. Drain eggs in colander and run under cold water to cool.

5. While eggs cool, slice and pit avocado. Scoop flesh into medium mixing bowl. Add relish, mustard, salt and spices.
6. Crack eggs shells and peel. Add boiled eggs to medium mixing bowl.
7. Using a fork, mash ingredients together until smooth mixture with soft chunks forms.
8. Remove *Sandwich Bread* from oven and let cool about 5 minutes.
9. Slice bread and fill with *Avocado Egg Salad*.
10. Serve immediately. Or refrigerate about 20 minutes and serve chilled.

# Sandwich Bread

Prep Time: 5 minutes

Cook Time: 15 minutes

Servings: 6

INGREDIENTS

2 cups almond flour

4 eggs

1/2 cup coconut cream (or melted cacao butter)

1/2 cup arrowroot powder (or tapioca flour)

1/3 cup ground chia seed (or flax meal)

1/4 cup coconut oil

2 tablespoons unsweetened applesauce

1 teaspoon apple cider vinegar

1 teaspoon baking soda

1/2 teaspoon sea salt

INSTRUCTIONS
1. Preheat oven to 350 degrees F. Lightly coat 6 mini round cake pans with coconut oil.
2. Beat eggs, coconut oil, coconut cream, applesauce and vinegar in medium mixing bowl with hand mixer or whisk.
3. In large mixing bowl, sift together almond flour, arrowroot, chia meal, baking soda and salt. Pour egg mixture into flour mixture and mix until well combined.

4. Pour batter into prepared mini cake pans and bake for about 15 minutes, or until golden brown and toothpick inserted comes out clean.
5. Remove from oven and let cool at least 5 minutes.
6. Slice in half and serve with your favorite deli meats or sandwich salads.

NOTE: Lightly oil medium loaf pan and bake for about 25 minutes for **Sandwich Bread** loaf.

# Sugar-Free Orange Kelp Noodle Salad

Prep Time: 5 minutes

Cook Time: 5 minutes

Servings: 2

INGREDIENTS

1 package (12 oz) kelp noodles

1/2 lemon

1 small cucumber

1 small red bell pepper

1 large carrot

Small bunch cilantro

2 large basil leaves

*Orange Avocado Dressing*

1 avocado

1 large orange

1/2 lemon

5 large basil leaves

1/4 teaspoon ground black pepper

1/4 teaspoon cayenne pepper or red pepper flake (optional)

Large bunch cilantro

INSTRUCTIONS

1. Rinse and drain kelp noodles. Add to medium bowl and soak 5 minutes in warm water and juice of 1/2 lemon. Or bring medium

pot of water with juice of 1/2 lemon to a boil and cook kelp noodles for 5 minutes, if softer texture preferred.
2. Peel, seed and cut cucumber in half width-wise. Cut bell pepper in half, then remove stem, seeds and veins. Use vegetable peeler or grater to make long, thin slices of carrot. Thinly slice cucumber and bell pepper lengthwise.
3. Add veggies and drained kelp noodles to medium mixing bowl.
4. For *Orange Avocado Dressing*, add basil and cilantro leaves to food processor or bullet blender with juice of orange and process to break down leaves. Slice avocado in half and remove pit. Scoop flesh into processor with juice of 1/2 lemon, black pepper and hot pepper (optional). Process until thick and until creamy.
5. Pour *Orange Avocado Dressing* over sliced veggies and kelp noodles. Toss to coat.
6. Serve immediately. Or refrigerate for 20 minutes and serve chilled.

# Zucchini Salad with Sundried Tomato Sauce

Prep Time: 20 minutes*

Servings: 2

INGREDIENTS

1 medium zucchini

1 tomato

5 sundried tomatoes

1 garlic clove

2 fresh basil leaves

1 tablespoon raw virgin coconut oil (or 2 tablespoons warm water)

1/4 teaspoon ground white pepper (or black pepper)

1/4 teaspoon sea salt

INSTRUCTIONS

1. Run zucchini through spiralizer, slice into long, thin shreds with knife, or use vegetable peeler to make flat, thin slices. Sprinkle with a pinch of salt and pepper, and gently toss to coat.
2. Add tomato, sundried tomatoes, peeled garlic, basil, coconut oil or warm water, and remaining salt and pepper to food processor or bullet blender. Process until sauce of desired consistency forms.
3. Transfer zucchini pasta to serving bowls. Top with tomato sauce and serve immediately.
4. Or refrigerate for 20 minutes and serve chilled.

# Quick Raw Avocado Slaw

Prep Time: 10 minutes*

Cook Time: 20 minutes

Servings: 4

INGREDIENTS

1/2 head cabbage (2 cups shredded)

1 avocado

1 carrot

Zest of 1 lemon

Juice of 1 lemon

1 tablespoon raw honey

2 tablespoons apple cider vinegar

1 teaspoon ground white pepper (or black pepper)

1 teaspoon sea salt

INSTRUCTIONS

1. Cut avocado in half and remove pit. Scoop flesh into large mixing bowl and mash with fork.
2. Remove any tough outer leaves and core from cabbage. Shred cabbage and carrot. Add to bowl with vinegar, honey, salt and pepper. Zest *then* juice lemon, and add.
3. Toss to combine.
4. Serve immediately. Or and place in refrigerator for 20 minutes and serve chilled.

# Vegetarian Texas Chili

Prep Time: 10 minutes*

Servings: 2

INGREDIENTS

5 - 6 plum tomatoes

1/2 teaspoon dried cumin

1/4 teaspoon chili powder

1/4 teaspoon onion powder

1/4 teaspoon garlic powder

1 teaspoon fresh oregano leaves  (or 1/4 teaspoon dried oregano)

1/2 teaspoon ground black pepper

1/4 teaspoon cayenne pepper or red pepper flakes (optional)

1  teaspoon Celtic sea salt

1 teaspoon chia seed (or flax seed)

1/2 cup raw cashews

Water

INSTRUCTIONS

1. *Soak raw cashews in enough water to cover overnight in refrigerator. Drain and rinse. Set aside.
2. Grind chia or flax in food processor or  high-speed blender. Set aside.
3. Juice tomatoes. Or add to food processor or high-speed blender and process. Add enough water to reach desired consistency, if necessary. Then strain.

4. Add tomato juice, ground chia or flax, 1/2 of soaked cashews, salt, pepper and spices to blender. Process until smooth, about 1 - 2 minutes.
5. Stir in remaining soaked cashews.
6. Pour into serving bowls and serve immediately.

# Caesar Salad

Prep Time: 10 minutes

Servings: 1

INGREDIENTS

2 cups chopped romaine lettuce

*Almond Parmesan*

1/4 cup raw almonds

1 teaspoon raw apple cider vinegar

1 teaspoon nutritional yeast (optional)

1/4 teaspoon garlic powder

1/4 teaspoon onion powder

1/4 teaspoon dried oregano

1/4 teaspoon Celtic sea salt

*Caesar Dressing*

2 tablespoons raw cashews (or raw sunflower seeds)

2 tablespoons raw sunflower seeds

1 tablespoon raw pine nuts (or raw sesame seeds or raw tahini)

2 tablespoons lemon juice

1 teaspoon sweetener*

1 garlic clove

3/4 teaspoon coconut aminos (or nutritional yeast)

1/2 teaspoon dried dill (optional)

Cracked or ground black pepper, to taste

Water

## INSTRUCTIONS

1. Rinse, dry and plate romaine lettuce.
2. For *Almond Parmesan*, add almonds, vinegar, salt, spices and nutritional yeast (optional) to food processor or high-speed blender. Process until almonds are coarsely ground and resemble ground parmesan cheese. Set aside.
3. For *Caesar Dressing*, peel garlic and add to food processor or high-speed blender with sweetener and lemon juice. Process until smooth. Then add remaining ingredients and process until smooth, about 1 - 2 minutes. Add enough water to reach desired consistency.
4. Drizzle *Caesar Dressing* over salad and sprinkle with *Almond Parmesan*. Serve immediately.

*\* raw honey or dried dates*

# Spiced Walnut Autumn Salad

Prep Time: 10 minutes

Servings: 1

INGREDIENTS

*Salad*

2 cups red lettuce leaves (or other colorful lettuce variety)

1/2 cup arugula

1/2 ripe pear

*Spiced Walnuts*

1/4 cup walnuts (halves or pieces)

1 tablespoons raw honey (or 1 dried date plus 1 tablespoon water)

1/4 teaspoon ground cinnamon

1/8 teaspoon ground ginger

1/4 teaspoon fresh ground nutmeg

1/8 teaspoon vanilla

1/4 teaspoon ground cardamom (optional)

*Orange Vinaigrette*

1 orange

2 tablespoons raw apple cider vinegar

2 teaspoons sweetener*

1 teaspoon raw walnut oil (or coconut, almond, sesame oil, etc.)

1 teaspoon raw tahini or sesame seeds (optional)

1 teaspoon ground mustard seeds (or whole mustard seeds)

1/4 teaspoon cracked or ground black pepper

INSTRUCTIONS
1. For *Salad*, rinse, dry and plate lettuce and arugula. Slice pear in half, and remove seeds. Top greens with sliced pears.
2. For *Spiced Walnuts*, process date and water in food processor or high-speed blender until smooth and add to small mixing bowl, if using. Or combine walnuts, spices and raw honey in small mixing bowl. Sprinkle over *Salad*.
3. For *Orange Vinaigrette*, zest and juice orange. Add to food processor or high-speed blender with vinegar, sweetener, spices and tahini (optional) and process until smooth, about 1 minute.
4. Drizzle *Orange Vinaigrette* over salad and serve immediately.

*stevia, raw honey or dried dates*

# Pecan Apricot Spinach Salad

Prep Time: 10 minutes

Servings: 1

INGREDIENTS

*Salad*

2 cups spinach leaves

1/2 cup chopped kale leaves

4 - 5 dried apricots

3 tablespoons pecans (halves or pieces)

*Honey Mustard Vinaigrette*

2 tablespoons raw honey (or 2 dried dates + 2 tablespoons water)

2 tablespoons ground mustard (or mustard seed)

2 tablespoons raw apple cider vinegar

3 tablespoons raw oil (coconut, walnut, almond, sesame, etc.)

3/4 teaspoons Celtic sea salt

INSTRUCTIONS

1. For *Salad*, rinse, dry and plate spinach and kale. Chop dried apricots. Sprinkle apricots and pecans over greens.
2. For *Honey Mustard Vinaigrette*, add honey, mustard, vinegar, oil and salt to food processor or high-speed blender and process until smooth, about 1 minute.
3. Drizzle *Honey Mustard Vinaigrette* over salad and serve immediately.

# Southern Style Egg Salad

Prep Time: 5 minutes

Cook Time: 15 minutes

Servings: 4

INGREDIENTS

8 cage-free eggs

1 avocado

1 celery stalk

1/4 sweet onion

1/4 cup sweet pickle relish (or dill pickle relish + 1 tablespoon raw honey, agave or date butter)

1/4 cup organic mustard

2 teaspoons paprika

1/2 teaspoon ground black pepper

1/4 teaspoon Celtic sea salt

INSTRUCTIONS

1. Bring medium pot of lightly salted water to a boil. Leave enough room in pot for eggs.
2. Gently add eggs to hot water with tongs and cook about 10 minutes.
3. Drain eggs into colander in sink. Fill pot with cold water and add eggs back to pot. Let cold water run slowly over eggs in pot to cool.

4. Slice and pit avocado. Scoop flesh into medium mixing bowl. Thinly slice celery. Peel and finely dice onion. Add to mixing bowl with relish, mustard, salt and spices. Mix with large spoon to combine.
5. Crack cooled eggs and peel off shells. Add boiled eggs to medium mixing bowl.
6. Use a fork or knife to chop eggs. Use large spoon to mix and mash ingredients together until smooth mixture with soft chunks forms. Stir to combine.
7. Transfer to serving dish and serve immediately. Or refrigerate about 20 minutes and serve chilled.

# Pesto Tomato Caprese

Prep Time: 5 minutes

Servings: 2

INGREDIENTS

1 large yellow tomato

1 large red tomato

Small bunch fresh basil

Celtic sea salt, to taste

Crack or ground black pepper, to taste

*Basil Pesto*

2 cups basil leaves (packed)

1/4 cup raw pine nuts

1/2 - 1/3 cup raw oil (coconut, walnut, almond, sesame, etc.)

2 garlic cloves

1/2 lemon (or 1 tablespoon raw apple cider vinegar)

1/4 teaspoon Celtic sea salt

INSTRUCTIONS

1. For *Basil Pesto*, peel garlic and add to food processor or high-speed blender with squeeze of 1/2 lemon. Process until finely chopped. Add pine nuts, basil, oil and salt and process until finely ground, about 1 minute.
2. Slice tomatoes and plate in alternating colors. Sprinkle with salt and pepper. Chiffon basil leaves.

3. Spread *Basil Pesto* over tomato slices and top with fresh basil. Serve immediately.

# Cashew Crunch Kelp Noodle Salad

Prep Time: 10 minutes*

Servings: 2

INGREDIENTS

1 package (12 oz) kelp noodles

1/2 lemon

1/2 small red bell pepper

*Cashew Sauce*

1 cup raw cashews

1/2 small red bell pepper

1/2 lemon

1 tablespoon coconut aminos (or raw apple cider vinegar)

2 large basil leaves

1/2 teaspoon smoked paprika

1/2 teaspoon ground black pepper

1/2 teaspoon Celtic sea salt

1/4 teaspoon ground turmeric (optional)

1/4 teaspoon smoked chili powder (optional)

Water

INSTRUCTIONS

7. *Soak 3/4 cup cashews in enough water to cover at least 4 hours, or overnight in refrigerator. Drain and rinse.

8. Drain and rinse kelp noodles. Add to medium bowl with warm water and juice of 1/2 lemon. Set aside 5 minutes.
9. Cut bell pepper in half. Remove stem, seeds and veins and set half of pepper aside. Julienne (thinly slice) remaining bell pepper and add to medium mixing bowl.
1. For *Crunchy Cashew Sauce*, add soaked cashews, bell pepper, juice of 1/2 lemon, coconut aminos, basil, salt and spices to food processor or high-speed blender. Process until smooth, about 2 minutes. Add enough water to reach desired consistency. Set aside.
10. Drain kelp noodles and add to sliced bell pepper. Add *Cashew Sauce* and toss to coat. Transfer noodles to serving dishes.
11. Roughly chop remaining 1/4 cup cashews. Sprinkle noodles and serve immediately. Or refrigerate for 20 minutes and serve chilled.

# Dill Stuffed Tomatoes

Prep Time: 15 minutes*

Servings: 2

INGREDIENTS

4 medium tomatoes

1 celery stalk

1 small carrot

1 green onion (scallion)

1/3 cup sunflower seeds

1/2 red bell pepper

1/4 small red onion (or sweet onion)

1/2 teaspoon Celtic sea salt

*Dill Dressing*

1/2 cup raw cashews

1 tablespoon raw apple cider vinegar (or coconut aminos)

1 teaspoon ground mustard (or mustard seeds)

1/2 lemon

1 small garlic clove

2 sprigs fresh dill

1/2 teaspoon Celtic sea salt

1/4 teaspoon ground white pepper (or pinch ground black pepper)

Water

## INSTRUCTIONS

1. *Soak cashews in enough water to cover at least 4 hours, or overnight in refrigerator. Drain and rinse.
2. Cut tops off tomatoes and scoop out seeds. Set aside.
3. Finely dice celery and carrot. Slice green onion. Peel and dice onion. Add to medium mixing bowl. Remove stem, seeds and veins from bell pepper, then dice. Add to bowl with sprinkle of salt. Set aside.
4. For *Dill Dressing*, peel garlic and add to food processor or high-speed blender with soaked cashews, vinegar, mustard, squeeze of lemon, dill, salt and pepper. Process until smooth and creamy, about 1 - 2 minutes. Add enough water to reach desired consistency.
5. Pour *Dill Dressing* over chopped veggies. Toss to coat.
6. Plate hollowed tomatoes and stuff with *Dill Dressing* veggie mixture. Serve immediately.

# Squash Blossom Stuffers

Prep Time: 10 minutes*

Servings: 4

INGREDIENTS

16 squash blossoms

1/2 cup walnuts

1 avocado

1 small onion

1/2 sprig fresh dill

1/2 lemon

1/2 teaspoon dried thyme

1/2 teaspoon ground white pepper (or ground black pepper)

1/2 teaspoon Celtic sea salt

1 teaspoon dried tarragon (optional)

Water

INSTRUCTIONS
1. *Gently rinse blossoms and pat dry. Let air dry for 30 minutes.
2. Cut avocado in half and remove pit. Scoop flesh into food processor or high-speed blender with walnuts, dill, squeeze of lemon, salt, pepper and spices. Process until smooth, about 2 minutes. Add enough water to reach desired consistency.
3. Peel onion and mince. Add to small mixing bowl with avocado mixture. Mix to combine.
4. Spoon mixture into squash blossoms. Serve immediately.

# Sugar-Free Indian Egg Fried Rice

Prep Time: 10 minutes

Cook Time: 15 minutes

Servings: 2

INGREDIENTS

1/2 head cauliflower

4 cage-free eggs

1 small carrot

1/2 red bell pepper

1/2 yellow bell pepper

1/4 onion (yellow or white)

2 small green onions (scallions)

2 tablespoons pure fish sauce (or coconut aminos or liquid aminos)

1 tablespoon coconut aminos (or coconut vinegar or liquid aminos)

1 teaspoon raw honey (or date butter or agave)

1 teaspoon sesame oil (optional)

1 large garlic clove

1/2 piece fresh ginger

1/2 teaspoon red pepper flake

Celtic sea salt, to taste

Coconut oil (for cooking)

Water

## INSTRUCTIONS

1. Cut cauliflower into florets and add to food processor with shredding attachment to rice. Or finely mince cauliflower. Set aside.
2. Heat medium pan or wok over high heat. Lightly coat with coconut oil.
3. Whisk eggs in medium mixing bowl. Set aside.
4. Remove stems, seeds and veins from bell peppers, then julienne (thinly slice). Finely dice carrot. Slice green onions. Peel and mince garlic, ginger and onion.
5. Add red pepper flakes to hot oiled pan. Sauté until just cooked fragrant, about 30 seconds. Add garlic, ginger and onion and sauté about 1 minute.
6. Add cauliflower to hot pan. Sauté about 5 minutes, until cauliflower is golden and a bit softened.
7. Add carrot, peppers and 1/2 green onions. Cook another 2 - 5 minutes, until cauliflower is cooked through. Add a few tablespoons of water and cover with lid to steam, if desired.
8. Push veggies aside and make well (opening) in center of pan. Pour whisked eggs into well in center and carefully scramble until fully cooked, about 2 minutes. Mix eggs into veggies.
9. Remove from heat and transfer to serving dish. Sprinkle remaining green onions over dish and serve hot.

# Weeknight Dinners Cookbook

# Table of Contents

Chicken Satay

Naturally Sweetened Orange Chicken

Cashew Chicken

Spicy Hunan Beef and Broccoli

Meaty Texas Chili

Spicy Meatball Marinara

Highland Sheppard's Pie

Black Pepper Stew

Nuts & Turkey Burgers

Chicken Bruschetta

Herb Roasted Pork Tenderloin

Ground Beef Stuffed Peppers

Stuffed Cabbage in Tomato Sauce

Slow Cooker Beef Pot Roast

Slow Cooker Beef Burgundy

Sugar-Free Spicy Thai Soup

Sweet Potato & Bacon Soup

Parchment Baked Salmon

Chicken Fries with Garlic Aioli

Ethiopian Beef Stew

Veggie Musakhan

Braised Lamb in Tomato Sauce

Garlic Sesame Chicken

Stewed Chicken and Dumplings

Oven-Fried Chicken

Southern Liver and Onions

Spicy Oregano Cubes

French Country Coq Au Vin

Uptown Clam Chowder

Sugar-Free Holiday Baked Ham

# Chicken Satay

Prep Time: 10 minutes*

Cook Time: 25 minutes

Servings: 4

INGREDIENTS

16 oz (1 lb) boneless skinless chicken

12 wooden skewers (soaked in water for 1 hour)

*Marinade*

1 tablespoon pure fish sauce (or liquid aminos or coconut Aminos)

2 inch piece fresh ginger rot

1 garlic clove

*Satay Sauce*

13 oz (1 can) full-fat coconut milk

1/2 cup crunchy almond butter

1 tablespoon raw honey or agave nectar

1 tablespoon pure fish sauce (or tamari or coconut aminos)

1 teaspoon apple cider vinegar (or liquid aminos or coconut vinegar)

4 shallots

2 garlic cloves

2 inch piece fresh ginger root

2 small red chili peppers

1 1/2 tablespoons lime juice

Coconut oil (for cooking)

INSTRUCTIONS

1. *Cut chicken into 1 inch strips. For *Marinade*, peel and mince garlic and ginger. Add to medium mixing bowl with fish sauce and whisk. Add chicken and toss with until coated. Cover and set aside to marinate for 1 hour.
2. *Soak wooden skewers in water in shallow dish for 1 hour.
3. Heat medium pan or wok over medium heat and add 1 tablespoon coconut oil.
4. For *Satay Sauce*, peel and mince shallots, garlic and ginger. Slice peppers. Add to hot pan and sauté until softened, about 5 - 8 minutes.
5. Reduce heat to low. Add almond butter, coconut milk, honey, fish sauce, vinegar and lime juice. Whisk until blended. Gently simmer for 10 minutes. Remove from heat, but keep warm.
6. Preheat outdoor grill or griddle pan over medium-high heat. Lightly coat with coconut oil.
7. Pierce marinated chicken strips with soaked skewers. Pour some *Satay Sauce* over chicken and brush lightly with marinade brush to coat. Transfer remaining *Satay Sauce* to serving dish.
8. Grill chicken on preheated grill until just cooked through, about 3 minutes per side. Turn over skewers halfway through cooking. Do not overcook.
9. Remove skewers from heat and transfer to serving dish. Serve with *Satay Sauce*.

# Naturally Sweetened Orange Chicken

Prep Time: 10 minutes

Cook Time: 10 minutes

Servings: 2

INGREDIENTS

12 oz (3/4 lb) boneless skinless chicken

1/2 cup almond flour

1 teaspoon flax meal

1 cage-free egg

1 green onion (scallion)

1/4 teaspoon cayenne pepper

1/2 teaspoon paprika

1/2 teaspoon ground black pepper

1/2 teaspoon Celtic sea salt

Coconut oil (for cooking)

Water

*Orange Sauce*

3 oranges (or tangerines or Clementines)

2 tablespoons raw honey (or agave)

1 tablespoon tamari (or liquid aminos or coconut aminos)

1 small garlic clove

1/2 inch piece fresh ginger

1/4 teaspoon ground black pepper

Water

INSTRUCTIONS

1. For *Orange Sauce*, zest 2 oranges, *then* juice all oranges into small pot. Peel and mince garlic and ginger. Add to pot with honey, tamari and pepper. Add 1/2 cup water.
2. Heat small pot over medium heat and bring to simmer. Simmer until *Orange Sauce* is reduced by half, about 5 minutes. Stir frequently. Remove from heat and set aside.
3. Heat medium pan over medium-high heat. Lightly coat pan with coconut oil.
4. In a shallow dish, blend almond meal, flax meal, salt and spices.
5. Whisk egg and 1 teaspoon water in separate shallow dish.
6. Cut chicken into 1 inch pieces. Dip chicken into egg wash, then dredge in seasoned almond meal.
7. Carefully place coated chicken pieces into hot oil and fry about 2 - 3 minutes, until golden brown and cooked through. Turn with tongs halfway through cooking.
8. Drain cooked chicken on paper towel, then transfer to medium mixing bowl. Pour *Orange Sauce* over chicken and toss to coat. Transfer to serving dish.
9. Slice scallions and sprinkle over dish. Serve hot.

# Cashew Chicken

Prep Time: 5 minutes

Cook Time: 10 minutes

Servings: 2

INGREDIENTS

12 oz (3/4 lb) boneless skinless chicken

1/2 cup raw cashews

1/2 small onion (white or yellow)

1/2 red bell pepper

1/2 green bell pepper

1 small celery stalk

2 tablespoons tamari (or coconut aminos or apple cider vinegar)

1 teaspoon raw honey (or agave or date butter)

1 garlic clove

1/2 inch piece fresh ginger

1/4 teaspoon ground black pepper

1/2 teaspoon Celtic sea salt

Bacon fat or coconut oil (for cooking)

INSTRUCTIONS

1. Heat large pan or wok over medium heat. Lightly coat with bacon fat or coconut oil.
2. Peel and mince garlic and ginger. Remove seeds, stems and veins from peppers, then roughly chop. Dice carrot. Slice celery.
3. Roughly chop chicken and season with salt and pepper.

4. Add garlic and ginger to hot oiled pan or wok. Sauté about 1 minute, until fragrant. Add seasoned chicken add sauté until browned, about 2 minutes. Transfer chicken to small bowl and set aside.
5. Add veggies to hot oiled pan. Sauté until tender and lightly browned, about 2 minutes. Add tamari, honey and cashews. Sauté until veggies are just cooked, but still crisp.
6. Add chicken back to pan and heat until just cooked through, about 2 minutes.
7. Transfer to serving dish and serve hot.

# Spicy Hunan Beef and Broccoli

Prep Time: 20 minutes

Cook Time: 10 minutes

Servings: 2

INGREDIENTS

12 oz (3/4 lb) beef sirloin

1/2 head broccoli

2 carrots

1 tablespoon tamari (or coconut aminos)

1 tablespoon dry sherry (or pure fish sauce or apple cider vinegar)

1 garlic clove

1/2 inch piece fresh ginger

1/2 teaspoon sesame seeds (optional)

Coconut oil (for cooking)

*Sauce*

1 tablespoon Asian chili paste

3 teaspoons tamari (or coconut aminos)

3 teaspoons chicken broth (or beef broth)

3 teaspoons dry sherry (or pure fish sauce or apple cider vinegar)

1 teaspoon raw honey (or agave)

1/2 teaspoon arrowroot flour

1/2 teaspoon sesame oil

2 garlic cloves

1/4 teaspoon fresh ground black pepper

INSTRUCTIONS

1. Cut beef against the grain into thin slices. Add to small mixing with tamari and sherry. And toss to coat. Set aside to marinate for 20 minutes.
2. For Sauce, peel and mince garlic. Add to small mixing bowl with chili paste, tamari, broth, sherry, honey, arrowroot, sesame oil and pepper. Mix to combine. Set aside.
3. Roughly chop broccoli into pieces. Slice carrots diagonally. Peel and mince garlic and ginger. Set aside.
4. Heat medium pan or wok over medium heat. Add 1 tablespoon coconut oil to hot pan.
5. Add marinated beef to hot pan in single layer. Let sear 1 minute on each side, undisturbed. Transfer to medium dish and set aside.
6. Add 1 tablespoon coconut oil to hot pan. Add garlic and ginger and sauté about 1 minute. Add broccoli and carrots. Sauté until lightly browned and softened, about 3 - 4 minutes. Stir frequently.
7. Add beef back to pan with *Sauce* and sesame seeds. Sauté until veggies are tender and beef is cooked through, about 2 minutes.
8. Transfer to serving dish and serve hot.

# Meaty Texas Chili

Prep Time: 5 minutes

Cook Time: 40 minutes

Servings: 4

INGREDIENTS

16 oz (1 lb) lean grass-fed ground beef (or elk, bison, turkey or chicken)

15 oz (1 can) organic tomato sauce

29 oz (2 cans) organic diced tomatoes

1 cup water

1 cup cashews

1 small onion

1 bell pepper

2 cloves garlic

2 tablespoons chili powder

1 1/2 tablespoons smoked paprika (or paprika)

1 tablespoon ground cumin

1 teaspoon Mexican oregano (or dried oregano)

1 teaspoon ground black pepper

1/2 teaspoon cayenne pepper

1 teaspoon Celtic sea salt

1 tablespoon coconut oil

INSTRUCTIONS

1. Heat medium pot over medium-high heat. Add 1 tablespoon coconut oil to hot pan.

2. Peel onion and garlic. Remove stems, seeds and veins from bell pepper. Roughly chop and add to food processor or high-speed blender. Pulse until finely minced.
3. Add minced veggies to hot skillet and sauté for about 1 minute. Add ground beef and spices. Brown beef for about 5 minutes. Stir with whisk to break up meat well, or wooden spoon to keep beef chunkier.
4. Add whole cans of diced tomatoes and tomato sauce, and water. Stir to combine.
5. Bring to a simmer, then reduce heat to medium and cover pot loosely with lid to prevent splatter. Simmer about 30 minutes. Stir occasionally.
6. Remove from heat and transfer to serving dish. Use large serving spoon or ladle to serve hot.

# Spicy Meatball Marinara

Prep Time: 5 minutes

Cook Time: 20 minutes

Servings: 4

INGREDIENTS

*Meatballs*

16 oz (1 lb) lean ground meat (beef, pork, chicken, turkey, bison, or any combination)

3/4 cup almond flour

1 cage-free egg

1/2 small onion (white, yellow or red)

1/2 teaspoon garlic powder

1/2 teaspoon cayenne pepper

1 teaspoon dried parsley

1 teaspoon dried oregano

1 teaspoon paprika

1 teaspoon red pepper flakes

1 teaspoon ground black pepper

1 teaspoon Celtic sea salt

1 tablespoon coconut oil

1 sprig fresh basil (for garnish, optional)

*Tomato Sauce*

14.5 oz (1 can) organic diced tomatoes

8 oz (1 can) organic tomato sauce

1 garlic clove

1/2 teaspoon dried oregano

1/2 teaspoon dried basil

1/2 teaspoon red pepper flakes

1/2 teaspoon ground black pepper

1 teaspoon coconut oil

## INSTRUCTIONS

1. Heat large pan over medium heat. Add 1 tablespoon coconut oil to hot pan. Heat medium saucepan over medium heat. Add 1 teaspoon coconut oil.
2. For *Tomato Sauce*, peel garlic and mince. Add to medium saucepan and sauté until just golden, about 30 seconds. Add diced tomatoes, tomato sauce, salt and spices. Simmer about 5 - 10 minutes, stirring occasionally.
3. For *Meatballs*, peel onion process in food processor or high-speed blender, or finely grate.
4. Add to large mixing bowl. Add egg, ground meat, almond flour, spices and salt. Mix well with hands or large wooden spoon.
5. Form 24 meatballs with scoop or tablespoon, then roll in hands. Add meatballs to hot large pan and brown for 10 minutes. Turn with spatula or tongs to cook on all sides.
6. Add *Meatballs* to *Tomato Sauce* and simmer another 5 minutes.
7. Transfer *Meatballs* to serving dish. Top with simmering *Tomato Sauce*. Garnish with fresh basil (optional).
8. Serve hot.

# Highland Sheppard's Pie

Prep Time: 20 minutes

Cook Time: 60 minutes

Servings: 4

INGREDIENTS

*Meat Filling*

24 oz (1 1/2 lbs) grass-fed ground lamb (or beef, bison, elk, etc.)

1 cup chicken broth or stock ( or beef brother or stock, or red wine)

1 large onion (yellow or white)

2 carrots

6 - 10 asparagus stalks (about 1/2 cup chopped)

1/2 sweet potato (about 1/2 cup diced)

2 garlic cloves

1 tablespoon organic tomato paste

1 teaspoon tamari (or coconut aminos)

2 tablespoons tapioca flour (or arrow root powder)

1 sprig fresh rosemary

1 sprig fresh thyme

1/2 teaspoon ground black pepper (or ground white pepper)

1 teaspoon Celtic sea salt

Bacon fat or coconut oil (for cooking)


*Parsnip Topping*

4 medium parsnips

1/2 medium onion (yellow or white)

2 tablespoons cacao butter (or coconut oil)

2 cups water

3/4 teaspoon Celtic sea salt

1/2 ground white pepper (or ground black pepper) (optional)

## INSTRUCTIONS

1. Heat medium pot over medium heat. Add 2 tablespoons bacon fat or coconut oil to hot pot.
2. For *Meat Filling*, peel and mince garlic. Peel and chop onion. Dice carrots and sweet potato. Chop asparagus. Add to hot oiled pot and sauté about 5 minutes.
3. Add lamb, salt and spices to veggies. Brown lamb and sauté another 5 minutes. Whisk in tapioca flour and cook another minute.
4. Remove rosemary and thymes leaves from stems and add to pot with stock, tomato paste and tamari. Let simmer and thicken about 12 minutes.
5. Preheat oven to 400 degrees F. Heat large pan with lid over medium heat. Add butter or oil to hot pan.
6. For *Parsnip Topping*, peel and mince or finely grate onion. Add to hot pan and sauté until translucent and aromatic, about 2 minutes.
7. Peel and slice or chop parsnips. Add to onions with water. Increase heat to high and bring to a simmer. Cover pan loosely with lid. Cook parsnips partially covered until softened and most of the water has evaporated, about 10 minutes.

8. Pour parsnips and onions into food processor or high-speed blender. Process until thick, smooth mixture forms. Add enough water to reach desired consistency. Set aside.
9. Transfer *Meat Filling* to baking or casserole dish. Top with *Parsnip Topping*. Smooth over or create design with offset spatula or back of spoon.
10. Bake about 25 minutes, until *Parsnip Topping* is golden.
11. Remove from oven and let cool at least 10 minutes. Serve warm.

# Black Pepper Stew

Prep time: 15 minutes

Cook time: 3 hr 45 minutes

Serves: 6

INGREDIENTS

1 ½ lbs beef stew meat

1 onion

1 (14.5 oz) can no-salt added stewed tomatoes, undrained

¼ tsp Celtic sea salt

½ tsp ground black pepper

1 dried bay leaf

2 cups water

3 tbsp arrowroot powder

12 small sweet potatoes cut in half

30 baby-cut carrots

INSTRUCTIONS

1. Heat oven to 325 degrees. In a bowl, mix arrowroot in water and stir to a paste (if you're not using arrowroot, use 1 cup water instead). Cut the onion into 8 wedges and cut potatoes in half.
2. In ovenproof Dutch oven, mix beef, onion, tomatoes, Celtic sea salt, ground black pepper and bay leaf. Mix arrowroot-thickened water (or 1 cup water) into Dutch oven.
3. Cover and bake for 2 hours, stirring one time.

4. Stir in the potatoes and carrots. Cover and bake until beef and vegetables are tender, about 1 hr 45 min. Remove bay leaf and serve immediately, or chill 20 minutes and then serve.

# Nuts & Turkey Burgers

Prep time: 10 minutes

Cook time: 6-12 minutes

Servings: 4

INGREDIENTS

16 oz ground turkey

1 cup walnuts

2 cloves garlic

1 onion

¼ tsp chipotle chili pepper powder

¼ tbsp smoked paprika

¼ tsp ground black pepper

INSTRUCTIONS

1. Chop walnuts into smaller pieces, about ⅛" cubes. Mince garlic and chop onion into small pieces, about ¼" pieces.
2. Combine the above with ground turkey and add chipotle chili pepper powder, smoked paprika and ground black pepper. Knead it all together and separate into four patties.
3. Cook on the grill on high heat, flipping occasionally, until desired done-ness.

# Chicken Bruschetta

Prep time: 10 minutes

Cook time: 10 minutes

Serves: 4

INGREDIENTS

4 grass-fed chicken breasts

2 tomatoes

4 olives

2 onions

¼ tsp ground black pepper

1 cup roasted red pepper

3 tbsp extra virgin olive oil

INSTRUCTIONS

1. Dice the tomatoes, chop the olives and onions, and combine them with ground black pepper and 2 tbsp olive oil in a bowl and mix well into a bruschetta. Puree the roasted red pepper in a blender and set aside.
2. Combine the chicken with 1 tbsp extra virgin olive oil and cook in a pan over medium-high heat for 4 minutes, turn once, and cook another 4-6 minutes, removing from heat while still tender.
3. Place one piece of chicken on each plate and pour the roasted red pepper over each, adding bruschetta over the top. Garnish with basil and serve.

# Herb Roasted Pork Tenderloin

Prep Time: 10 minutes*

Cook Time: 15 minutes

Servings: 4

INGREDIENTS

1 pork tenderloin

1 teaspoon dried rosemary

1 teaspoon dried thyme

1 teaspoon dried oregano

1 teaspoon dried basil

1 teaspoon dried marjoram (optional)

1/2 teaspoon ground black pepper

1 teaspoon Celtic sea salt

*Apricot Sauce*

1 cup dried apricots

2/3 cup water

1 teaspoon apple cider vinegar (or dry white wine)

INSTRUCTIONS

1. Preheat oven to 425 degrees F. Heat small pan over medium heat.
2. Rub tenderloin with salt and spices, then press into meat so it adheres. Place on sheet pan, or wire rack over sheet pan.
3. Roast for 10 - 15 minutes, until just cooked through and no pink remains. Remove pork from oven and let rest 10 minutes.

4. For *Apricot Sauce*, add dried apricots, water and vinegar to food processor or high-speed blender. Process until smooth, about 1 - 2 minutes.
5. Add *Apricot Sauce* to hot pan and reduce until slightly thickened. Stir well and do not let burn. Remove from heat.
6. Slice pork and transfer to serving dish. Top pork with *Apricot Sauce* and serve warm.

# Ground Beef Stuffed Peppers

Prep Time: 10 minutes

Cook Time: 50 minutes

Servings: 4

INGREDIENTS

4 bell peppers

16 oz (1 lb) ground meat (beef, pork, chicken, turkey, etc.)

1/2 head cauliflower (1 cup riced)

1/2 cup roasted red peppers

1/4 cup sundried tomatoes

1/4 cup pecans

1/2 small onion (white, yellow or red)

2 tablespoons coconut oil

2 garlic cloves

Medium bunch fresh herbs (parsley, oregano, thyme, etc.)

1/4 teaspoon red pepper flakes

1 teaspoon ground white pepper (or black pepper)

1 teaspoon Celtic sea salt

Water

INSTRUCTIONS

1. Preheat oven to 350 degrees F.
2. Cut tops off peppers, then remove stems from tops and seeds and veins from bottoms of peppers. Leave bottoms of peppers hollow

but do not pierce. Place in baking dish just large enough to fit peppers snuggly. Set aside.
3. Peel onion and garlic. Roughly chop onions, garlic and cauliflower. Add to food processor or high-speed blender with pecans. Pulse about 15 seconds.
4. Add tops of peppers, roasted red peppers, sundried tomatoes, ground meat, salt, pepper, and fresh herbs to processor. Process until coarsely ground, about 1 - 2 minutes.
5. Use large spoon to stuff peppers with mixture. Add 1/2 cup water to bottom of baking dish. Cover peppers with aluminum foil.
6. Bake 30 minutes. Carefully remove foil and continue baking uncovered 10 - 20 minutes, until stuffing is golden brown and cooked through .
7. Carefully remove from oven and transfer peppers to serving dish. Serve hot.

# Stuffed Cabbage in Tomato Sauce

Prep Time: 15 minutes

Cook Time: 60 minutes

Servings: 6

INGREDIENTS

1 large cabbage head

*Filling*

2 1/2 lbs ground beef

4 cage-free eggs

1/2 onion (yellow or white)

1/3 cup almond flour

1/2 cup cauliflower (riced or minced)

1/2 teaspoon dried thyme

1/2 teaspoon ground black pepper (or ground white pepper)

1 1/2 teaspoons Celtic sea salt

*Tomato Sauce*

2 cans (15 oz) organic tomato sauce

1/2 cup golden raisins

1/2 onion (yellow or white)

2 tablespoons raw honey (or agave or date butter)

2 tablespoons apple cider vinegar

1 1/2 teaspoons Celtic sea salt

1 teaspoon ground black pepper (or ground white pepper)

2 tablespoons bacon fat (or coconut oil or ghee)

## INSTRUCTIONS

1. Preheat oven to 350 degrees F. Bring large pot of salted water to boil.
2. Carefully place cabbage head in boiling water for about 5 minutes. Use tongs to peel each layer of leaves from head as soon as they become tender. Set leaves aside on sheet pan to cool.
3. For *Tomato Sauce*, peel and mince onions. Add 1/2 of onions to medium mixing bowl. Add tomato sauce, honey, vinegar, raisins, salt and spices and mix to combine.
4. For *Filling*, add remaining onions to large mixing bowl. Mince or rice cauliflower and add to bowl with eggs, almond flour, salt, spices, and 1 cup *Tomato Sauce.* Mix well with hands or large wooden spoon.
5. Cut hard rib from bottom of each cooled cabbage leaf. Place 1/3 - 1/2 cup *Filling* near the bottom edge of cabbage leaf and roll into a neat package, tucking in sides as you roll. Repeat with remaining filling and cabbage.
6. Spread 1 cup *Tomato sauce* along bottom of deep, lidded baking dish. Place 1/2 the cabbage rolls in baking dish. Add 1/2 remaining sauce, the remaining cabbage rolls. Top with remaining sauce.
7. Tightly cover dish with lid and bake for 1 hour, until meat is cooked through and veggies are tender.
8. Transfer to serving dish and serve hot.

# Slow Cooker Beef Pot Roast

Prep Time: 20 minutes

Cook Time: 6 hours

Servings: 8

INGREDIENTS

5 lb bone-in beef pot roast (or bone-in beef chuck)

2 1/2 cups chicken stock (or broth)

1 1/2 cups button mushrooms (about 1/2 pint)

3 carrots

2 celery stalks

1 onion (white or yellow)

2 garlic cloves

2 1/2 tablespoons tapioca flour (or arrowroot powder)

1 tablespoon organic tomato paste

2 sprigs fresh thyme

1 sprig fresh rosemary

1 - 2 tablespoons ground black pepper

1 - 2 tablespoons Celtic sea salt

1 tablespoon ghee (or cacao butter)

2 tablespoons coconut oil (for cooking)

INSTRUCTIONS

1. Heat large skillet over medium-high heat. Add coconut oil to hot pan.

2. Generously season beef on all sides with salt and pepper. Sprinkle 1 tablespoon tapioca or arrowroot over beef and pat to coat. Add to hot oiled pan and sear on all sides until browned, about 5 minutes per side. Set aside in baking dish to rest.
3. Slice mushrooms. Peel and chop onions. Peel and mince garlic.
4. Add ghee or butter and mushrooms to hot pan. Sauté about 2 minutes.
5. Add onions and sauté until translucent, about 5 minutes. Add garlic and sauté about 1 minute.
6. Stir in remaining 1 1/2 tablespoons tapioca or arrowroot and cook about 1 minute. Stir in tomato paste.
7. Slowly stir in chicken stock and bring to simmer, about 5 minutes. Remove from heat.
8. Roughly chop carrots and celery. Add to bottom of slow cooker. Place rested beef over veggies and pour in any juices from beef. Add rosemary and thyme. Add mushroom mixture over beef.
9. Cover slow cooker with lid. Turn on to high and cook 5 - 6 hours, until beef is fork tender.
10. Turn off slow cooker and carefully remove lid. Skim off any fat from surface and remove bones.
11. Transfer to serving dish and serve hot.

# Slow Cooker Beef Burgundy

Prep Time: 30 minutes

Cook Time: 7 hours

Servings: 6

## INGREDIENTS

3 lbs boneless stew beef

2 cups beef stock (or broth)

1 bottle (750 ml) organic dry red wine

1/2 cup organic sparkling apple cider (or cognac)

8 oz (1/2 lb) nitrate-free bacon

1 pint fresh mushrooms (about 2 cups)

4 large carrots

2 yellow onions

2 cups whole pearl onions (peeled)

2 garlic cloves

1 tablespoon organic tomato paste

3 tablespoons tapioca flour (arrowroot powder)

1/2 teaspoon dried thyme

1 teaspoon ground black pepper

2 teaspoons Celtic sea salt

2 tablespoons coconut oil (for cooking)

## INSTRUCTIONS

1. Heat large skillet over medium-high heat. Add coconut oil to hot pan.

2. Cut beef into chunks than add to large mixing bowl. Season beef with salt and pepper, then add 2 tablespoons tapioca or arrowroot. Toss to coat.
3. Add seasoned beef to hot oiled pan in batches to brown, about 5 minutes per batch. Set aside in slow cooker.
4. Chop bacon and add to hot pan. Sauté until just crisp and fat renders out, about 5 - 8 minutes. Set aside in slow cooker.
5. Peel and chop yellow onions. Peel and mince garlic. Add to hot bacon grease and sauté about 5 minutes. Set aside in slow cooker.
6. Cut mushrooms in half. Add to hot pan with tomato paste, remaining tapioca or arrow root, thyme and apple cider. Stir to combine. Then add beef stock to deglaze pan. Bring to simmer, about 5 minutes.
7. Pour mushroom mixture into slow cooker. Add red wine and peeled pearl onions. Chop carrots and add to slow cooker. Stir to combine.
8. Cover slow cooker with lid. Turn on to low and cook 6 - 8 hours, until meat and veggies are tender.
9. Turn off slow cooker and carefully remove lid.
10. Transfer to serving dish and serve hot.

# Sugar-Free Spicy Thai Soup

Prep Time: 15 minutes

Cook Time: 1 hour

Servings: 4

INGREDIENTS

1 3/4 lbs boneless skinless chicken thighs

4 cups chicken broth (or stock)

1 can (14 oz) coconut milk (lite or full-fat)

1 1/2 cups white mushrooms

2 lemongrass stalks

1 small red onion

3 garlic cloves

3 inch piece ginger root

2 tablespoons pure fish sauce

1 1/2 teaspoons red curry paste

2 limes

1 jalapeño pepper

Small bunch cilantro

1 tablespoon coconut oil

Water

INSTRUCTIONS

1. Thinly slice bottom 2/3 of lemongrass. Peel chop garlic and ginger. Add to medium pot with chicken broth. Heat over medium-high-heat and bring to boil.

2. Reduce heat to low and simmer for 30 minutes. Strain liquid and reserve.
3. Heat pot over medium heat. Add coconut oil to hot pot.
4. Roughly chop chicken and add to hot oiled pot. Sauté and brown for 5 minutes. Quarter mushrooms and add to pot. Sauté for 5 minutes.
5. Stir in red curry paste, fish sauce, and juice of 1 lime. Add reserved chicken broth and coconut milk. Stir to combine and bring to a simmer.
6. Reduce heat to low and simmer 15 - 20 minutes. Skim off and discard any excess fat that rises to the top.
7. Peel and slice red onion. Add to pot and stir. Cook about 5 minutes, until onion softens.
8. Remove from heat. Roughly chop add 1/2 to pot and stir to combine.
9. Slice jalapeño into rings and cut lime into wedges.
10. Transfer to serving dish. Sprinkle remaining cilantro and jalapeño slices over dish.
11. Serve hot with lime wedges.

# Sweet Potato & Bacon Soup

Prep Time: 20 minutes

Cook Time: 1 hour 20 minutes

Servings: 4

INGREDIENTS

4 cups chicken broth (or veggie broth)

2 large sweet potatoes (yams)

8 oz (1/2 lb) nitrate free bacon

1 cup full-fat coconut milk

1/4 teaspoon cayenne pepper

1/2 teaspoon ground cinnamon

1/2 teaspoon dried thyme

1 teaspoon ground black pepper

Celtic sea salt, to taste

INSTRUCTIONS

1. Preheat oven to 400 degrees F. Line sheet pan with parchment or baking mat.
2. Cut sweet potatoes crosswise into thick slices and lay on prepared sheet pan. Sprinkle with salt and pepper, to taste.
3. Roast sweet potatoes for about 45 minutes, until golden brown and cooked through. Remove from oven and allow to cool slightly. Then remove skin from sweet potatoes.
4. Heat medium pot over medium-high heat.

5. Chop bacon and add to hot pot. Sauté bacon until crisp, about 7 - 8 minutes. Remove bacon and set aside.
6. Add bacon fat to food processor or high-speed blender with peeled sweet potatoes and broth. Process until puréed.
7. Or add peeled sweet potatoes and broth to pot and purée in with immersion blender.
8. Add spices and coconut milk and stir to combine. Reduce heat to medium and let simmer about 10 minutes.
9. Transfer to serving dish and sprinkle with crisp bacon. Serve hot.

# Parchment Baked Salmon

Prep Time: 5 minutes

Cook Time: 20 minutes

Servings: 1

INGREDIENTS

8 oz salmon fillet (deboned, skin-on)

6 - 8 medium asparagus stalks

1/2 lemon

1 basil sprig

1 rosemary sprig

1 teaspoon coconut oil

Pinch black pepper

Pinch sea salt

Parchment paper

Kitchen twine

INSTRUCTIONS

1. Place large sheet pan on bottom rack of oven. Preheat oven to 400 degrees F. prepare parchment sheet.
2. Place salmon in middle of parchment sheet skin-side down and sprinkle with salt and pepper. Place asparagus stalks next to salmon. Cut lemon into thin slices and place over fish and asparagus. Rub herbs between palms, then lay basil and rosemary sprig over lemon slices. Drizzle 1 teaspoon coconut oil over salmon and asparagus.

3. Gather edges of parchment up over salmon and tie tightly with kitchen twine to form sealed pouch.
4. Place pouch directly on hot baking sheet in hot oven. Bake for 20 minutes.
5. Remove from oven and carefully transfer pouch to serving plate. Carefully open pouch to release steam.
6. Serve hot.

# Chicken Fries with Garlic Aioli

Prep Time: 10 minutes

Cook Time: 15 minutes

Servings: 2

INGREDIENTS

8 oz boneless, skinless chicken breast

1 egg

1/2 cup almond meal

1 teaspoon flax meal (or ground chia seed)

1 teaspoon ground black pepper

1/2 teaspoon paprika

1/2 teaspoon onion powder

1/2 teaspoon garlic powder

1/2 teaspoon chili powder

1/2 teaspoon sea salt

*Garlic Aioli*

1/2 - 3/4 cup coconut oil

1 egg yolk

2 garlic cloves

1/2 small lemon

1/4 teaspoon ground white pepper (or black pepper)

1/4 teaspoon sea salt

3 tablespoons flavorful oil (black truffle, walnut, almond, sesame, etc.) (optional)

INSTRUCTIONS

1. Heat large pan over medium-high heat and coat with coconut oil.
2. For *Garlic Aioli*, peel garlic and add to food processor or blender with egg yolk, juice of 1/2 lemon, salt and pepper. Process until smooth, scraping down sides of vessel.
3. While processor or blender is running, very slowly drizzle in enough coconut oil to create thick mayo-like mixture. Drizzle in flavorful oil as well will processor runs (optional). If mixture is runny, drizzle in more coconut oil while processor runs until thickened. Pour into serving dish and refrigerate.
4. Slice chicken into half width-wise, creating twice the fillets. Try to slice at thickest portion to keep all fillets equal thickness.
5. Slice chicken fillets into long, 1/2 inch wide strips. Place strips between two paper towels and press to absorb excess moisture.
6. In a shallow dish, blend almond meal, flax or chia meal, spices and salt.
7. Beat egg in small mixing bowl. Toss chicken strips in beaten egg to lightly coat, then dredge in seasoned almond meal.
8. Carefully place coated chicken strips into hot oil and fry about 2 - 3 minutes, until golden brown and cooked through. Turn with tongs half way through cooking.
9. Drain cooked chicken on paper towel, then transfer to serving dish.
10. Serve hot with *Garlic Aioli*.

# Ethiopian Beef Stew

Prep Time: 30 minutes

Cook Time: 1 hour

Servings: 4

INGREDIENTS

24 oz (1 1/2 lb) stew beef

2 cups beef stock (or chicken or veggie stock)

2 tablespoons organic tomato paste

1/2 teaspoon raw honey (or agave or date butter)

1 small onion

2 garlic cloves

2 teaspoons Celtic sea salt

2 teaspoons *Spice Blend*

2 tablespoons ghee (or cacao butter or bacon fat)

3 tablespoons coconut oil (or bacon fat)

*Spice Blend*

1/8 teaspoon ground nutmeg

1/8 teaspoon ground allspice

1/8 teaspoon turmeric

1/4 teaspoon ground cumin

1/4 teaspoon ground cinnamon

1/4 teaspoon ground cloves

1/4 teaspoon garlic powder

1/2 teaspoon ground black pepper

1/2 teaspoon ground fenugreek

1/2 teaspoon ground ginger

1/2 teaspoon ground coriander

1/2 teaspoon cardamom seed (or 1/4 teaspoon ground cardamom)

1 teaspoon dried onion flakes (or 1/2 teaspoon onion powder)

1 tablespoon paprika

2 tablespoons red pepper flakes

INSTRUCTIONS

1. Heat medium pot over medium-high heat. Add Spice blend and toast until fragrant. Stir frequently and do not burn. Remove toasted *Spice Blend* and set aside.
2. Add ghee and coconut oil to hot pot.
3. Cut beef into 1 inch chunks. Set aside.
4. Peel onion and garlic. Mince garlic and dice onion. Add to hot oiled pot and sauté until caramelized, about 2 - 3 minutes.
5. Add tomato paste, 2 teaspoons *Spice Blend* and honey to pot. Stir and cook into thick paste, about 2 minutes. Stir in a few tablespoon of beef stock to loosen paste.
6. Add beef, remaining beef stock and salt to pot. Stir to combine. Reduce heat to medium-low and simmer until beef is tender and sauce thickens and reduces, about 1 hour. Stir occasionally.
7. Transfer to serving dish and serve room temperature.

# Veggie Musakhan

Prep time: 4 minutes

Cook time: 8 minutes

Servings: 4

INGREDIENTS

4 pieces grass-fed chicken thighs

1 onion

2 cloves garlic

3/4 cup sliced carrots

2 handfuls Kale greens

2 tbsp chinese five spice

2 tbsp smoked paprika

2 tbsp chipotle chili pepper powder

1 tbsp olive oil

2 tsp lemon juice

1 tbsp coconut oil

INSTRUCTIONS

1. Mince garlic and chop onion to desired size (medium strips work best). Chop carrots to 1/4" thickness. De-rib the kale and chop it coarsely, wash it and allow water to remain on the leaves. Bring 4 cups of water to a light boil.
2. Heat 1 tbsp olive oil over medium heat in a large pan. Add carrot and onion and cook for 8 minutes, stirring occasionally.

3. Meanwhile, heat 1 tbsp coconut oil over medium heat in a separate pan. Add chicken and cook for 4 minutes. Season chicken with chinese five spice, chipotle chili pepper powder and smoked paprika and turn, adding more of each spice to the other side of the chicken, cooking for another 4 minutes or until cooked through.
4. Add kale to boiling water and boil until bright green, about 5 minutes. Remove from water and let sit while the vegetables and chicken continue cooking.
5. Add everything into the pan with the vegetables and add 2 tsp lemon juice. Add minced garlic and stir for 1 minute.
6. Serve immediately.

# Braised Lamb in Tomato Sauce

Prep Time: 20 minutes

Cook Time: 9 hours

Servings: 4

INGREDIENTS

3 lbs bone-in lamb shank

1 can (15 oz) organic tomato sauce

1 can (15 oz) organic crushed tomatoes

1/4 cup red wine (or apple cider vinegar)

2 cups pearl onions (peeled)

2 garlic cloves

1 teaspoon dried oregano

1 teaspoon dried thyme

1 teaspoon paprika

1 teaspoon ground black pepper

2 teaspoons Celtic sea salt

1 tablespoon coconut oil (for cooking)

Chicken stock (or water)

INSTRUCTIONS

1. Heat medium skillet over medium-high heat. Add coconut oil to hot pan.
2. Add lamb to hot oiled pan and sear on all sides, about 3 - 4 minutes per side. Set aside in slow cooker.

3. Peel pearl onions. Peel and mince garlic. Add to hot oiled pan and sauté about 2 minutes.
4. Add tomatoes sauce, red wine or vinegar, salt and spices to pan. Stir to combine.
5. Add to slow cooker with crushed tomatoes enough chicken stock or water to cover lamb.
6. Cover slow cooker with lid. Turn on to medium and cook 4 - 5 hours, until meat is tender.
7. Turn off slow cooker and carefully remove lid.
8. Transfer to serving dish and serve hot.

# Garlic Sesame Chicken

Prep Time: 10 minutes

Cook Time: 20 minutes

Servings: 2

INGREDIENTS

12 oz (3/4 lb) boneless skinless chicken

1/4 cup almond flour

1/4 cup arrowroot powder

1 large cage-free egg white

2 teaspoon sesame seeds

1/4 teaspoon cayenne pepper

1/2 teaspoon garlic powder

1/2 teaspoon ground black pepper

1/2 teaspoon Celtic sea salt

Coconut oil (for cooking)

*Garlic Sauce*

1/2 yellow onion

1/2 lemon

6 garlic cloves

1/4 inch piece fresh ginger

1/4 cup date butter (or raw honey or agave)

2 tablespoons pure fish sauce

2 tablespoons coconut aminos (or tamar or liquid aminos)

2 tablespoons tamari (or liquid aminos or coconut aminos)

1/4 teaspoon ground black pepper

Water

## INSTRUCTIONS

1. For *Garlic Sauce*, peel onions, garlic and ginger. Roughly chop and add to food processor or high-speed blender. Add date butter, fish sauce, coconut aminos, tamari and black pepper. Process until smooth.
2. Add sesame seeds to small pot. Heat over medium heat and toast about 2 minutes. Stir constantly. Transfer to small bowl and set aside.
3. Pour *Garlic Sauce* into pot and cook until onions and date butter until caramelized and garlic is fragrant, about 5 minutes. Stir frequently.
4. Add enough water to create saucy consistency. Stir frequently and bring to simmer. Simmer until *Garlic Sauce* is reduced by half and browned, about 5 minutes. Remove from heat and set aside.
5. Heat medium pan over medium-high heat. Coat pan with about 1/4 inch coconut oil.
6. In a shallow dish, blend almond meal, arrowroot powder, salt and spices.
7. Beat egg whites in small mixing bowl with hand mixer or whisk until light and frothy, about 2 - 4 minutes.
8. Cut chicken into 1 inch pieces. Dip chicken in egg whites, then dredge in seasoned flour mixture.
9. Carefully place coated chicken pieces into hot oil and fry about 2 - 3 minutes, until golden brown and cooked through. Turn with tongs halfway through cooking.

10. Drain cooked chicken on paper towel, then transfer to medium mixing bowl. Pour *Garlic Sauce* and 1 teaspoon toasted sesame seeds over chicken and toss to coat. Transfer to serving dish.
11. Sprinkle remaining toasted sesame seeds over dish. Serve hot.

# Stewed Chicken and Dumplings

Prep Time: 10 minutes

Cook Time: 1 hour 20 minutes

Servings: 4

INGREDIENTS

2 lb whole chicken (innards removed)

6 - 10 cups water

3 carrots

3 celery stalks

1 small white onion (or yellow onion)

4 bay leaves

1 1/2 tablespoons dried thyme (or 4 sprigs fresh thyme)

1/2 teaspoon dried oregano

1 teaspoon paprika

2 teaspoon ground black pepper

1 tablespoon Celtic sea salt

*Dumplings*

3 cups almond flour

1/2 cup arrowroot powder

2 cage-free egg

1/2 cup coconut oil, chilled (or coconut or cacao butter, room temperature)

1/2 teaspoon baking soda

1/4 teaspoon ground bay leaf

1 teaspoon dried thyme

1/2 teaspoon ground white pepper (or ground black pepper)

1 teaspoon Celtic sea salt

Nut milk (or chicken broth or stock)

## INSTRUCTIONS

1. Heat large pot over medium-high heat. Place chicken breast-down in hot pot. Sear chicken and turn to brown and render out fat for about 15 minutes.
2. Chop carrots and celery. Peel onion and mince. Add to chicken with salt and spices. Sauté about 2 minutes.
3. Add enough water to pot to cover chicken. Increase heat to high and bring to a boil. Reduce heat to medium and simmer about 30 minutes. Place lid loosely over pot to prevent splatter, if necessary.
4. For *Dumplings*, sift almond flour and arrowroot into medium mixing bowl. Cut in solid oil or butter with fork until crumbly mixture forms. Add egg, salt and spices, baking soda, and enough nut milk or chicken broth from pot to bring together soft, slightly sticky dough.
5. Carefully remove chicken from pot with long utensil and set aside. Use utensils to remove skin from chicken. Carve chicken into desired pieces and place back in back.
6. Use spoon or scoop to gently drop dough into pot. Cover with well-fitting lid and let simmer about 15 - 20 minutes, until *Dumplings* and chicken are cooked through. Gently stir soup to periodically prevent *Dumplings* from sticking. Turn over any *Dumplings* that are not submerged.
7. Remove from heat and transfer to serving dish. Serve hot.

# Oven-Fried Chicken

Prep Time: 10 minutes

Cook Time: 60 minutes

Servings: 4

INGREDIENTS

32 oz (2 lb) bone-in, skinless chicken

3/4 cup fine almond flour

3/4 cup coarse almond meal (or almond flour)

2 cage free eggs

1/3 cup nut milk

1/2 teaspoon cayenne pepper

1 teaspoon ground black pepper

1 1/2 teaspoons paprika

1 1/2 tablespoons Celtic sea salt

Coconut oil (in spray bottle)

INSTRUCTIONS

1. Preheat oven to 350 degrees F. Fill spray bottle with warm coconut oil.
2. Line sheet pan with aluminum foil. Place metal cooling or baking rack over lined sheet pan. Generously spray metal rack with coconut oil to coat. Set second sheet pan aside.
3. Add almond meal and/or flour to small mixing bowl with 1 tablespoon salt and spices. Mix to combine with fork or whisk to break up clumps.

4. In shallow dish, beat eggs and nut milk until combined.
5. Use serving spoon or measuring cup to dust second sheet pan with layer of almond flour mixture onto. Sprinkle chicken with 1/2 tablespoon salt.
6. Dip and coat all chicken pieces in egg mixture then lay on second sheet pan, over layer of almond flour mixture. Use spoon or measuring cut to sprinkle almond flour mixture from mixing bowl over dipped chicken. Pat almond flour mixture into chicken on all sides until well coated.
7. Transfer coasted chicken to prepared wire rack. Generously spray coated chicken with coconut oil.
8. Bake 60 - 70 minutes, until coating is crisp and chicken is cooked through. Remove from oven and allow to cool at least 10 minutes. Then place crispy chicken on paper towels to drain, if desired.
9. Transfer to serving dish and serve immediately.

# Southern Liver and Onions

Prep Time: 20 minutes*

Cook Time: 25 minutes

Servings: 4

INSTRUCTIONS

20 oz (1 1/4 lb) calves liver

2 onions (yellow or white)

4 slices nitrate-free bacon

1 lemon

2 tablespoons arrowroot powder

1/2 teaspoon Celtic sea salt

1/2 teaspoon cracked black pepper (or ground black pepper)

Bacon fat or coconut oil (for cooking)

INSTRUCTIONS

1. *Remove thin outer membrane from liver and slice into 1/4 inch fillets. Add to glass container. Juice lemon into container and toss to coat. Cover well and refrigerate overnight.
2. 2. Heat large cast-iron pan or skillet set over medium heat.
3. Cut bacon lengthwise into long, thin strips. Then cut in thirds crosswise and add to hot pan. Sauté bacon and let crisp, about 5 minutes. Stir occasionally. Decrease heat to medium-low.
4. Peel and thinly slice onions. Add to bacon and sauté until caramelized, about 10 minutes. Stir occasionally. Remove caramelized onions and bacon from pan and set aside.

5. Drain liver fillets in colander in sink. Rinse under running water, then pat dry.
6. In shallow dish, add arrowroot powder, salt and pepper. Mix with fork to combine.
7. Dredge liver slices in arrowroot mixture and shake off excess. Place coated liver fillets on a plate and coat remaining liver fillets.
8. Add 2 tablespoons bacon fat or coconut oil to hot pan. Add single layer of coated liver to hot oiled pan and sear for 1 minute per side. Place liver on paper towel to drain. Repeat with remaining liver.
9. Transfer liver to serving dish. Top with caramelized onions and bacon. Serve immediately .

# Spicy Oregano Cubes

Prep time: 1 hr 10 minutes

Cook time: 16-20 minutes

Serves: 4

INGREDIENTS

1 boneless leg of lamb

5 tbsp extra virgin olive oil

2 tsp dried oregano

1 tbsp fresh parsley

1 lemon

½ eggplant

4 small onions

2 tomatoes

5 fresh bay leaves

¼ tsp Celtic sea salt

¼ tsp ground black pepper

INSTRUCTIONS

1. Cube the lamb, chop the fresh parsley, juice the lemon, slice and quarter the eggplant into thick pieces, halve the onions and quarter the tomatoes.
2. Place lamb in a bowl. Mix olive oil, oregano, parsley, lemon juice and Celtic sea salt and ground black pepper. Pour this over the lamb and mix well. Cover and marinate for 1 hour.

3. Preheat the grill. Thread the marinated lamb, eggplant, onions, tomatoes and bay leaves in evenly on each of four skewers.
4. Place the kebabs on a grill inside a grill pan and brush them evenly with the leftover marinade until the marinade is all gone. Cook over medium heat turning once the kebabs once, for about 8-10 minutes on each side, basting them whenever enough juice collects in the bottom of the grill pan.
5. Serve immediately or chill 20 minutes and then serve.

# French Country Coq Au Vin

Prep Time: 30 minutes

Cook Time: 7 hours

Servings: 6

1 (5 - 7 lb) stewing chicken (innards removed)

2 cups chicken stock (or broth)

2 bottles(750 ml) organic red wine

6 oz nitrate-free bacon

2 cups button mushrooms

1 medium onion (yellow or white)

2 celery stalks

2 carrots

2 cups pearl onions (peeled)

3 garlic cloves

2 tablespoons organic tomato paste

1/4 cup tapioca flour (arrowroot powder)

6 sprigs fresh thyme

1 bay leaf

1 teaspoon ground black pepper

2 teaspoons Celtic sea salt

2 tablespoons coconut oil (for cooking)

INSTRUCTIONS

1. Heat large skillet over medium-high heat. Add coconut oil to hot pan.

2. Chop or cube bacon and add to hot pan. Sauté until just crisp and fat renders out, about 5 - 8 minutes. Set aside in slow cooker.
3. Cut chicken into on-the-bone serving pieces (legs, wings, thighs, breasts). Then add to large mixing bowl. Season chicken with salt and pepper, then add tapioca or arrowroot. Toss to coat.
4. Shake off excess flour and add seasoned chicken to hot greased pan in batches to brown, about 4 minutes per side. Set aside in slow cooker.
5. Peel and quarter yellow or white onion. Peel and smash garlic. Quarter mushrooms. Add to hot pan and sauté about 5 minutes. Set aside in slow cooker.
6. Cut carrots and celery into quarters. Add to hot pan with peeled pearl onions, tomato paste, remaining tapioca or arrowroot, and chicken stock. Stir to combine and deglaze pan. Bring to simmer, about 5 minutes.
7. Pour mixture into slow cooker. Add red wine, bay leaf and fresh thyme. Stir to combine.
8. Cover slow cooker with lid. Turn on to low and cook 6 - 8 hours, until meat and veggies are tender.
9. Turn off slow cooker and carefully remove lid. Remove celery, carrot, thyme and bay leaf.
10. Transfer to serving dish and serve hot.

# Uptown Clam Chowder

Prep Time: 10 minutes

Cook Time: 1 hour 15 minutes

Servings: 4

INGREDIENTS

24 - 36 medium live littleneck clams (or other clam varieties)

2 cans (11.5) organic tomato juice (or about 6 large tomatoes)

2 cans (14.5 oz) organic crushed tomatoes

2 medium carrots

2 medium celery stalks

2 medium parsnips

1 red bell pepper

1 tablespoon tamari (or coconut aminos or liquid aminos)

1 bay leaf

1/4 teaspoon cayenne pepper

1/2 teaspoon onion powder

1 tablespoon dried oregano

1 tablespoon dried basil

1 teaspoon dried thyme

1 teaspoon ground black pepper

Celtic sea salt, to taste

1 cup clam juice (or veggie or chicken stock, or water) (optional)

INSTRUCTIONS

1. Have fishmonger shuck clams. Or carefully shuck clams yourself. Reserve clam juice. Set aside in refrigerator.
2. Juice tomatoes, if using. Add tomato juice and crushed tomatoes to medium pot. Heat pot over high heat.
3. Remove seeds, stems and veins from bell pepper. Dice bell pepper, carrot, celery, and parsnips. Add to pot with spices and salt, to taste.
4. Bring pot to boil, then reduce heat to low. Place lid loosely over pot to prevent splatter. Simmer for 45 minutes. Stir occasionally.
5. Remove lid and stir. Add clam juice, stock or water to reach desired consistency (optional).
6. Remove clams from refrigerator and chop, if desired. Add clams and juice to pot. Stir to combine.
7. Replace lid and continue cooking about 20 - 30 minutes. Stir occasionally.
8. Transfer to serving dish and serve hot.

# Sugar-Free Holiday Baked Ham

Prep Time: 10 minutes

Cook Time: 5 hours

Servings: 12

INGREDIENTS

1 (12 lb) bone-in ham

1 (20 oz) can organic pineapple rings (in juice)

1/2 cup date butter (or raw honey or agave)

1/2 cup whole cloves

1/2 cup water

1 lemon

1 lime

1 orange

About 12 pitted cherries (optional)

Toothpicks (optional)

INSTRUCTIONS

1. Preheat oven to 325 degrees F.
2. Drain pineapple juice into small mixing bowl. Juice lemon, lime and orange into bowl. Add sweetener and water. Mix well.
3. Place ham in roasting pan and score rind in crosshatch (diamond) pattern with knife.
4. Press cloves into rind. Place cherries on rind and secure with toothpick. Hang pineapple rings on cherries.

5. Pour pineapple juice mixture over ham and bake uncovered 4 - 5 hours, until internal temperature reaches 160 degrees F. Baste with juices about every 30 minutes.
6. Remove ham from oven. Remove toothpicks and carve. Serve hot.

Printed in Great Britain
by Amazon